KNIGHTS AND CASTLES

GROOVY TUBE BOOK

Fact Book • Chess Pieces • Game Board

by Kate Torpie

Illustrated by Thomas Denmark

Conceived, developed, and designed by
the creative team at innovativeKids®
Game by innovativeKids®
Copyright © 2008 by innovativeKids®
All rights reserved

Published by innovativeKids®
A division of innovative USA, Inc.
18 Ann Street, Norwalk, CT 06854
iKids is a registered trademark in
Canada and Australia

ISBN 13: 978-1-58476-726-8
Not for individual sale
10 9 8 7 6 5 4 3 2 1

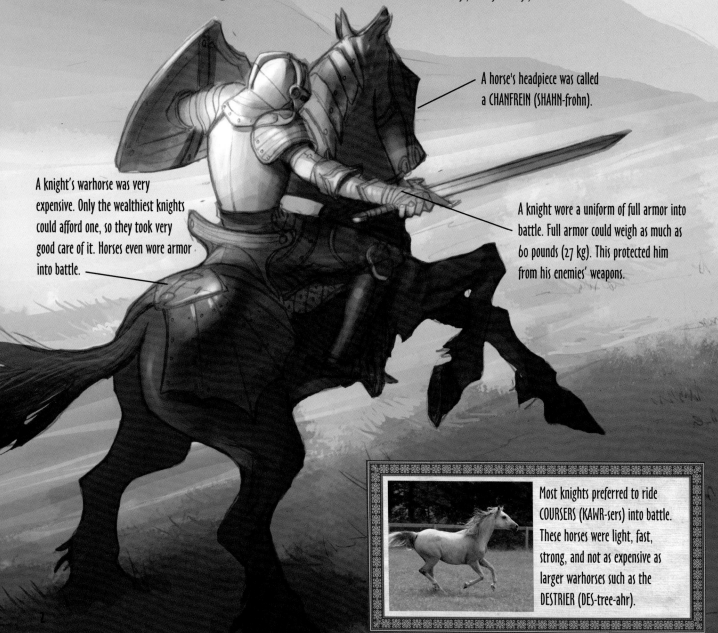

In medieval times, fierce armies of knights fought for kings and rich landowners. A knight never directly refused any favor asked of him by his king or other leaders. He was an extraordinary soldier and gentleman. Knights are famous for their bravery, loyalty, and honor.

A horse's headpiece was called a CHANFREIN (SHAHN-frohn).

A knight's warhorse was very expensive. Only the wealthiest knights could afford one, so they took very good care of it. Horses even wore armor into battle.

A knight wore a uniform of full armor into battle. Full armor could weigh as much as 60 pounds (27 kg). This protected him from his enemies' weapons.

Most knights preferred to ride COURSERS (KAWR-sers) into battle. These horses were light, fast, strong, and not as expensive as larger warhorses such as the DESTRIER (DES-tree-ahr).

The only way to identify a knight in full armor was by the coat of arms on his shield.

Knights trained special warhorses for battle. These horses were not scared by battle noises or afraid of swords. Some were even taught to bite and kick.

The pattern on a shield is called a COAT OF ARMS. This knight's shield is purple, which symbolizes royalty and justice. The dots, called FURS, show that this knight is from a dignified family. The bear shows that his family is strong and clever.

3

Being knighted was an honor. A king might choose to honor a brave soldier by knighting him, but most of the time, knights came from noble families that had money and power. Young boys who would become knights were sent away from home for training.

The first step in becoming a knight was to serve as a page. At the age of about seven, a page began to learn to ride a horse and to use weapons. From the women of the household, he learned manners. A page also helped with chores around the house and learned important social skills, such as how to dance and play chess.

A talented page could become a squire when he turned 14. Then, he served one knight. He woke the knight and made his meals. He helped the knight dress in his armor, and he cleaned the knight's armor after battles. He even tended to the knight when he was injured. A squire learned to ride a horse by battling wooden targets called QUINTAINS (KWIN-tains) and spent his free time honing his sword fighting skills.

During a ceremony called THE ACCOLADE, the king dubbed a man a knight by tapping his shoulder with his own sword. Some squires never became knights because they weren't skilled enough or weren't rich enough to buy armor and horses.

Afterward, noble ladies helped the knight dress in his new armor.

5

A knight was expected to live by a strict set of rules known as the Code of Chivalry. The code stated that a knight should be brave, generous, and humble. A good knight fought injustice wherever he found it. A knight was supposed to fall in love with one woman—even if she was married to another man. Some knights were troubadours; they wrote songs and poems for their ladies. The woman would give her knight a token, such as her handkerchief, which he would wear.

According to legend, one knight wore a dress belonging to a lady he loved instead of armor. He was badly injured while fighting. The lady's husband honored the knight by throwing a party. The lady wore the bloodstained dress to show her appreciation.

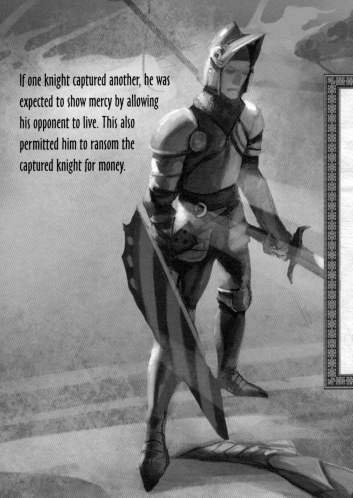

If one knight captured another, he was expected to show mercy by allowing his opponent to live. This also permitted him to ransom the captured knight for money.

The Ten Commandments of Chivalry

Thou shalt believe all that the Church teaches, and shalt observe all its directions.

❖

Thou shalt defend the Church.

❖

Thou shalt respect all weaknesses, and shalt constitute thyself the defender of them.

❖

Thou shalt love the country in the which thou wast born.

❖

Thou shalt make war against the Infidel without cessation, and without mercy.

Thou shalt not recoil before thine enemy.

❖

Thou shalt perform scrupulously thy feudal duties, if they be not contrary to the laws of God.

❖

Thou shalt never lie, and shall remain faithful to thy pledged word.

❖

Thou shalt be generous, and give largess to everyone.

❖

Thou shalt be everywhere and always the champion of the Right and the Good against Injustice and Evil.

Excerpted from "Chivalry" by Leon Gautier

A knight was expected to follow the rules of chivalry, even during battles. There were no sneak attacks. Commanders set a time and place for a battle. The Church even demanded that knights never fight on Sundays.

A wound could be a death sentence for a knight. With no proper medical care available, wounds often turned into deadly infections.

Tournaments were a source of entertainment for the castle and a way for knights to make money. Weapons were rounded so as not to kill. Tournaments could last as long as a month. One popular game was jousting. The joust began as armored opponents charged on horseback, lances upright. Riders then lowered their lances and tried to strike and "unhorse" each other. The losing knight often paid the winner with his horse, his armor, and his weapons.

Many lords and knights held tournaments to show off their wealth. They provided food and drink for everyone for weeks at a time. In the evenings, the knights would dine and dance with the guests.

Sometimes lances broke or accidentally poked through an opponent's helmet. For this reason, FROG-MOUTH HELMETS were worn.

Knights in a joust often approached each other at combined speeds of about 60 mph (100 km/hr). (That's faster than the speed limit on many highways today!) A knight earned three points for knocking his opponent off his horse and two points for striking his opponent on the shoulder or helmet hard enough to break his lance.

If a knight wanted to seem mysterious, he would show up without a coat of arms.

Even local peasants were allowed to attend.

A wooden barrier called a TILT separated opponents.

Because there was less chance of injury, the armor a knight wore at a tournament was very different from the armor he wore into battle. It was more decorative, and it protected only the side where his opponent was supposed to hit him.

It took a team of workers to create one suit of armor. A full suit of armor was very expensive. It could take a knight ten months to earn back the money he needed for his armor! Medieval knights wore suits made of plate armor. They weighed about 60 pounds (27 kg). Most weapons could not puncture the armor. A knight was helped into his armor by his squire. Underneath their armor, knights wore thickly padded clothes and CHAIN MAIL, a mesh garment of small metal rings. Getting dressed could take more than an hour.

The BESAGEW (beh-sah-GOO) blocked the knight's armpits from lances or spears.

The BREASTPLATE protected a knight from being struck in the chest or heart.

The POLEYN (pole-EHN) covered the knight's knees. Like gauntlets, poleyns were made of small movable iron plates.

GAUNTLETS kept a knight's hands safe. Many small movable plates allowed a knight to move his hands easily.

ARMING A KNIGHT

The greaves (shins)

Cuisse & poleyn (knees & upper arms)

Arming doublet (padded jacket)

Chain mail (neck and groin)

Breastplate (chest)

The face guard on the CLOSE-HELMET protected the knight. It could be lifted or closed, depending on which was needed most—better vision or better protection.

The LANCE REST gave a knight relief from the weight of his lance.

Horses needed protection in battle, too. A full coat of horse armor was called a BARD. Because of the weight of the bard, a horse could only move at a slow trot when wearing it.

A knight needed extra long STIRRUPS so he could almost stand as he rode his horse.

Backplate (back and hips)

Spaulders (upper arms)

Coutler (elbow defenses)

Gauntlets (hands)

Helmet (head)

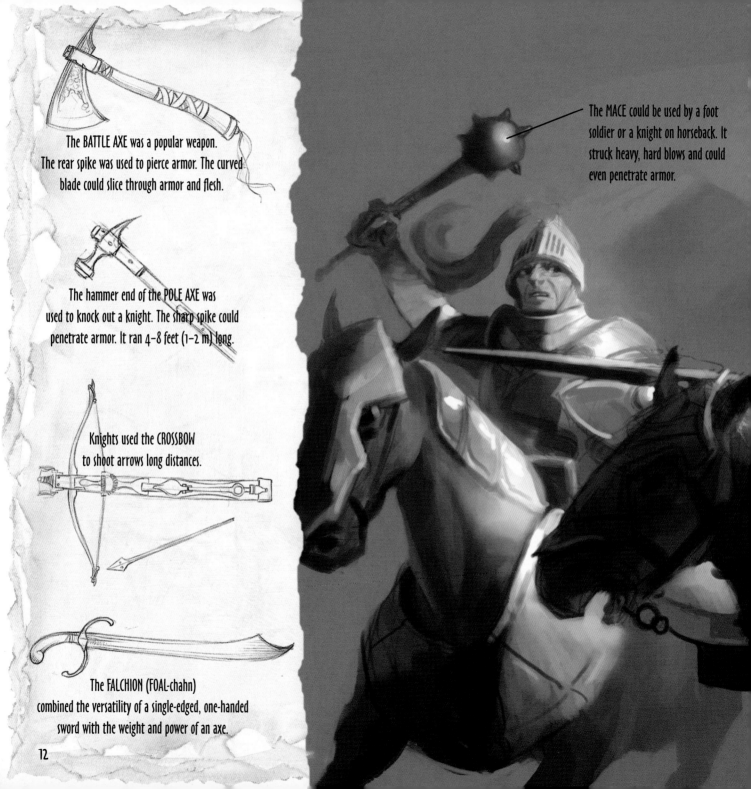

The BATTLE AXE was a popular weapon. The rear spike was used to pierce armor. The curved blade could slice through armor and flesh.

The hammer end of the POLE AXE was used to knock out a knight. The sharp spike could penetrate armor. It ran 4–8 feet (1–2 m) long.

Knights used the CROSSBOW to shoot arrows long distances.

The FALCHION (FOAL-chahn) combined the versatility of a single-edged, one-handed sword with the weight and power of an axe.

The MACE could be used by a foot soldier or a knight on horseback. It struck heavy, hard blows and could even penetrate armor.

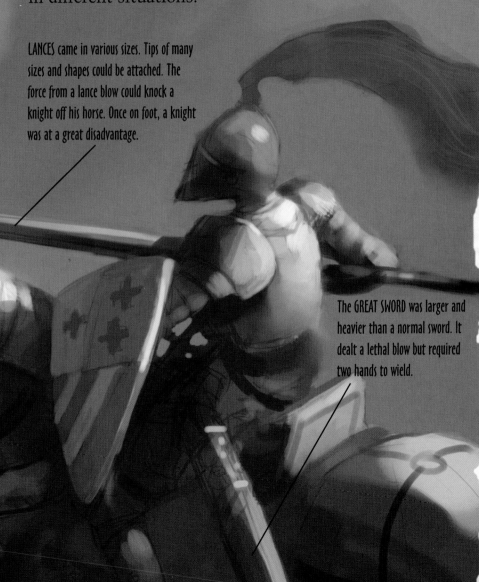

Knights fought hand-to-hand or on horseback. A knight's life depended on having weapons that were deadly and easy to use. Though a sword was the most common weapon for a knight to carry, every knight favored certain weapons and used different ones in different situations.

LANCES came in various sizes. Tips of many sizes and shapes could be attached. The force from a lance blow could knock a knight off his horse. Once on foot, a knight was at a great disadvantage.

The GREAT SWORD was larger and heavier than a normal sword. It dealt a lethal blow but required two hands to wield.

A WAR HAMMER had a heavy, sharp tip designed to penetrate even the thickest armor. It is like the pole axe but smaller for close combat.

As a knight rode into battle, he threw pointed JACKS towards the enemy's battlefield. If a horse stepped on a jack, it would buck its rider.

When a knight swung the FLAIL above his head, it gained momentum and power. If swung wrong, it could land a deadly hit on the wrong target—the knight swinging it.

RONDEL DAGGERS were small enough to penetrate chain mail.

13

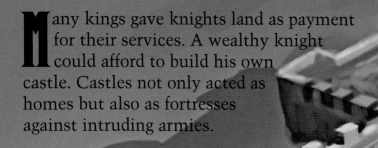

Many kings gave knights land as payment for their services. A wealthy knight could afford to build his own castle. Castles not only acted as homes but also as fortresses against intruding armies.

A GREAT HALL was used for feasts. Kitchens were huge and had two or three fireplaces—each big enough to roast a pig! The owner of the castle slept in a feather bed with silk covers. The floors were covered with sweet-smelling herbs and straw.

The GATEHOUSE was the easiest area to attack because it was the main entrance through the outer wall. Inside was a PORTCULLIS (port-KUHL-uhs), a gate that could be dropped quickly to stop intruders.

ROUND TOWERS allowed guards to look out in all directions and were stronger than towers with corners.

From the WALL-WALK, guards had a good view of anyone approaching.

The DRAWBRIDGE was the main way in or out of the castle. It could be shut tight during an invasion.

The MOAT surrounding a castle was filled with water to prevent enemies from easily reaching the castle walls.

A guard could shoot arrows through narrow holes in the wall called ARROW LOOPS.

During a siege, a family could take refuge inside the KEEP, the central tower in a castle. Necessities like food and water were stored inside.

In the floor, there were secret trap doors that led to the worst kind of prison: an OUBLIETTE (oo-blee-EHT). Most oubliettes were below ground so that they would flood when it rained, making survival nearly impossible.

Guards used toilets in small rooms within the towers. They were simple chutes that emptied into the moat. Toilets in the keep were fancier. They emptied into a chamber pot. Servants then emptied the pots into the moat.

15

Building a castle took a lot of time, money, and workers. One famous castle, Dover Castle in England, took ten years to complete. Materials needed to build a castle, such as stone and wood, were brought in on horse-drawn carts from places miles away. It could take as many as 2,000 people to build a castle!

Windsor Castle has seen many renovations since it was built in the 1100s. The castle boasts over 1,000 rooms! It has survived two sieges, a fire, and the air raids of World War II. In the 1500s, when the Plague spread, Queen Elizabeth I ordered anyone who tried to enter the castle to be hanged! The British royal family lives there today.

This blacksmith forges the metal bars to fit over windows. He will also make a chain for the system that opens and closes the drawbridge.

These men are digging the moat around the castle.

A crowbar is used to move stones into their proper places.

Heavy baskets of stone are hoisted to workers atop the wall using a pulley.

Quarrymen remove stone and load it into horse-drawn carts. Masons cut the stone into usable shapes. It might take a year to add ten feet of height to a wall.

The mason uses a mallet and chisel to carve decorations into stone.

The Tower of London is one of the most famous castles in the world. It has more than 21 towers protecting it! The White Tower at the Tower of London was the home to kings and queens but was most famous for the prisons within its walls. Important prisoners were tortured or killed there. Three English queens were held there before being beheaded. When King Edward IV died in 1483, his two sons, ages 12 and 9, were imprisoned there by enemies who wanted to steal the throne. The little princes disappeared, never to be seen again.

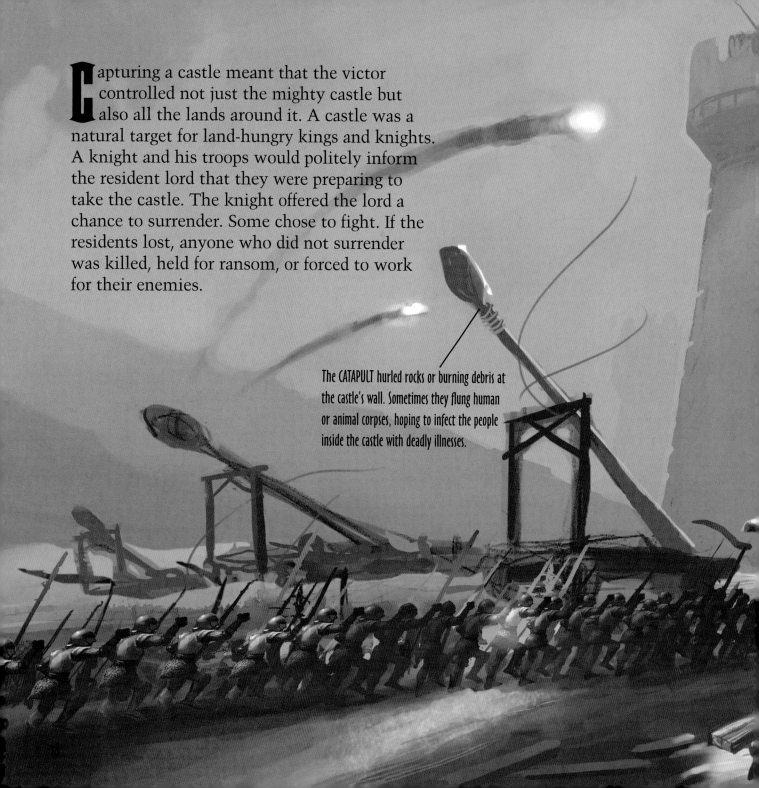

Capturing a castle meant that the victor controlled not just the mighty castle but also all the lands around it. A castle was a natural target for land-hungry kings and knights. A knight and his troops would politely inform the resident lord that they were preparing to take the castle. The knight offered the lord a chance to surrender. Some chose to fight. If the residents lost, anyone who did not surrender was killed, held for ransom, or forced to work for their enemies.

The CATAPULT hurled rocks or burning debris at the castle's wall. Sometimes they flung human or animal corpses, hoping to infect the people inside the castle with deadly illnesses.

Some soldiers placed ladders on the walls and simply attempted to climb over the wall.

Soldiers used a BATTERING RAM to slam the castle doors and gates in hope of weakening them to the point of collapse.

These towers, called BELFRIES, were built on site by invading armies. A belfry had a drawbridge that could be lowered atop the castle walls to allow invaders easy entry.

To MINE castle walls, men dug tunnels under them. They placed wood supports in the tunnel then lit the wood on fire. Once the supports collapsed, so would the walls.

Sometimes an invading army waited out the residents, camping outside so residents could not leave for food or other goods. Invaders waited for people to starve or for the well inside the castle to run dry. In 1346, the English launched a siege at Calais (Cal-LAY), France. Instead of attacking the fortress, they waited it out. Hundreds of people inside the castle, including women and children, died of starvation. Finally, after 11 months, the lord of the castle surrendered.

Defending a castle was a matter of life and death. The longer an attacking army waited for a castle's surrender, the more bloodthirsty the besieged inhabitants became. The inhabitants knew they faced death or imprisonment if they were defeated.

Castle defenders hurled burning objects at a belfry.

Castle guards would throw pots of boiling water and oil at invaders from atop the wall-walk.

Most gatehouses were built with murder holes through which guards could pour boiling oil or Greek fire on invaders.

Guards shot arrows at their attackers.

Guards placed a pot of water at the corner of each tower. If the enemy was mining under the wall, the water in the pot would ripple.

Throwing a dead animal out made the intruders think the residents inside had plenty of food. If the hungry attackers were desperate enough to eat an old carcass, they might get sick. As many knights died from diseases as they did from battle injuries.

By the time the castle was penetrated, those inside and outside were angry and ready for war. Frustrated knights had no mercy for the defenders—and the terrified castle guards fought for their lives.

GREEK FIRE burned even when doused with water. No one knows what the formula was for this terrible weapon.

Enemies might lay siege to a knight's castle while he was away, leaving it up to the lady of the castle to organize the castle's defense strategy.

Battles in medieval days were different from battles and wars fought now. In medieval wars, both sides agreed on a time and date for the battle. When armies of knights battled, it was often for control of a city.

1099, Valencia, Spain: "El Cid," a Spanish knight whose nickname meant "the lord" in Arabic, fought this last battle while dead. According to legend, El Cid cemented his reputation as a brave knight when he fought Muslim invaders in Valencia. During battle, an arrow struck and killed him. But this didn't stop El Cid. His soldiers strapped El Cid to his horse and sent him charging again at the enemy! It worked; the Spanish won the battle.

1487, Stoke, England: Henry VII took the English throne from the ruling family, the Yorks. The only remaining York heir was kept locked in an oubliette in the Tower of London. However, a look-alike of the heir, Lambert Simnel, surfaced. Some powerful allies took him to Ireland, dubbed him the righteous king of England, and returned to wage war on King Henry's army. The impostor's army lost, but King Henry pardoned him in an act of mercy.

1066, Hastings, England: On the night before a battle between the English and Normans (French), the English army stayed up drinking and eating. The next morning, when they awoke, they were surprised to see the Norman army retreating from the battlefield. It was a trick. The English army chased after them and fell out of order. The Normans used their confusion to turn on them and win!

1346, Crécy, France: A small English army of about 10,000 defended itself against a French army with more than three times as many men. King John of Bohemia (bo-HEE-mee-ah) helped the English cause——even though he had long ago gone blind. He asked two knights to lead him so that he could strike a blow against the enemy. The king and his knights fought bravely and advanced so far forward that their bodies were not found until the next day. The English won the battle. Crécy was also one of the first battles in which a longbow and arrows were used. Some consider this to be the end of chivalry on the battlefield.

23

Stories about knights have always been popular, but which are true, and which are just legends? Decide for yourself which of the following tales are true. The answers are at the bottom of the page.

St. Joan of Arc

In the 1400s, a French girl named Joan insisted she heard a voice from heaven telling her to dress as a knight. She convinced the king of France to let her lead his army against the English. When she was captured, the king of France betrayed Joan by making no effort to rescue her. After a lengthy trial, Joan of Arc was burned alive.

Sir John Conyers Falchion

In the 1300s, a dragon known as "The Sockburn Worm" terrorized the English town of Durham. Townspeople complained that it ate all their livestock. Sir John Conyers Falchion bravely killed the dragon with a weapon of his own invention.

Ulrich von Lichtenstein

This Austrian knight led a quest to honor his love. He set out across Europe challenging any knight he met to a joust in honor of his lady. He wore a helmet with a crest of Venus, the goddess of love, and he may have even dressed as her during his quest!

King Arthur and the Knights of the Round Table

King Arthur was an English king who embodied the Code of Chivalry. Normally, a king sits at the head of his table. Arthur asked his favorite knights to sit at a round table with him to show he considered them his equals. Arthur's most trusted knight, Lancelot, eventually betrayed him by running off with his wife, Guinevere.

William Wallace

Considered a rebel by the English, Wallace led the Scots against a better-armed, better-trained English army. After his victory, he was knighted by the Scottish king. He was later betrayed and turned over to the English, and he suffered a gruesome traitor's death at their hands.

True. Joan of Arc was later named a saint by the Catholic church.

False. While the falchion, a single-edged, one-handed sword, got its name from this legend, dragons do not exist.

True. Lichtenstein even wrote a book of poems about his adventures. Its title translates to "Service of the Lady."

False. King Arthur may be based on a real Celtic king, but Arthur, Lancelot, and Guinevere are all characters in the story of "King Arthur and the Knights of the Round Table."

True. The life of William Wallace was the basis for the film "Braveheart."